Prayers Before a River

Prayers Before a River

A Beginner's Guide to Prayer

John C. Maher

RESOURCE *Publications* • Eugene, Oregon

PRAYERS BEFORE A RIVER
A Beginner's Guide to Prayer

Copyright © 2021 John C. Maher. All rights reserved. Except for brief quotations in critical publications or reviews, no part of this book may be reproduced in any manner without prior written permission from the publisher. Write: Permissions, Wipf and Stock Publishers, 199 W. 8th Ave., Suite 3, Eugene, OR 97401.

Resource Publications
An Imprint of Wipf and Stock Publishers
199 W. 8th Ave., Suite 3
Eugene, OR 97401

www.wipfandstock.com

PAPERBACK ISBN: 978-1-7252-7483-9
HARDCOVER ISBN: 978-1-7252-7479-2
EBOOK ISBN: 978-1-7252-7484-6

12/21/20

Unless otherwise indicated, all Bible quotations are taken from the Holy Bible, English Standard Version® (ESV®), copyright © 2001 by Crossway, a publishing ministry of Good News Publishers. Used by permission. All rights reserved.

To my father and mother, who taught me how to pray

Atomriug indiu, niurt nime,
soilsi gréne, étrochtai éscai

I arise today, through the virtue of heaven
The bright light of the sun, The radiance of an evening moon.

—"ST. PATRICK'S BREASTPLATE" OR "THE DEER'S CRY,"
IRISH, CA. FIFTH CENTURY

Contents

Acknowledgements | xi
Preface | xiii

1. On Praying | 1

2. Prayers | 11

    Prayer before a River: Continuity Is Strength | 11
    Prayer of the Bereaved: Into the Main of Light | 12
    Prayer of the Insomniac: Fixing the Noise in My Life | 13
    Prayer for the Animals: God's Loved Creatures | 14
    Prayer of a Sick Person: Reviewing Life | 15
    Prayer of a Parent: Loving with a Broken Heart | 16
    Prayer of a Worker: Building Creation | 17
    Prayer of an Agnostic: God Means Nothing, and Something | 18
    Prayer of a Person in Love: Actually | 19
    Prayer for No More War: Wisdom Is Compassion | 20
    Prayer for Friendship: Lies, Strength, Trust | 20
    Prayer of an Unrepentant Sinner: Honor Your Imperfections | 21
    Prayer before a Christmas Tree: The Dignity of Nature | 22
    Morning Prayer | 23
    Night Prayer | 24

Prayer of the Faiths: Border Work | 24
Prayer of a Texter: AG Can We Text? | 25

3. On Praying | 27

4. Prayers | 36

Prayer to an All-Gendered God: Beyond Words | 36
Prayer against Pessimism: Dark Mind, Bright Heart | 37
Prayer of a Liar: Take Me Up | 38
Prayer for Hope: A Unique Wisdom | 39
Prayer for My Religion: Goodness and Misery | 39
Prayer of a Mother and Father: The Grace of Children | 40
Prayer of a Person Who Cannot Pray:
  Keeping in Touch with Eternity | 41
Prayer of the Unemployed: The Work of My Hands | 42
Prayer of an Administrator: Following the Mission | 43
Prayer before Mess: Kondo-ing My Spiritual Life | 44
Prayer of the Traveler: Each Journey Is a Pilgrimage | 44
Prayer before Meals | 45

5. On Praying | 46

6. Prayers | 52

Prayer of a Dying Person: Gratitude | 52
Prayer of a Student: The Beat Goes On | 53
Prayer of a Homeless Person: Give Us a Future | 54
Prayer of an Addict: Roads to Freedom | 54
Prayer of a Single Parent: My Child Inspires Me | 55
Prayer of the Body: Feelin' Good | 56
Prayer of Joy: A Life Worth Loving | 56
Prayer to the Holy Spirit: Switching Me On | 57
Prayer of an Envious Person: Turning to Thankfulness | 58
Prayer of a Person Harassed:
  Freedom from Domination | 59

Prayer of Dismay about Government:
 Best Practice in the Family of Nations | 60
Prayer of a Person Who Lost Faith:
 Walking Away, Walking Back | 61

Bibliography | 63

Acknowledgements

I OWE A SPECIAL debt of gratitude to Michael Piret and his guidance, amidst the quiet and beauty of Magdalen College Chapel, Oxford. I am deeply grateful to John Bruce Gillingham for his inspiration and good counsel. I am indebted to Howard Brook for his comments and renewed friendship as well as to Beverley Curran for helpful comments and ever-collegial encouragement. I appreciate Peter Groves and also Jonathan Jong at St Mary Magdalen, Oxford, for sharing with me the gift of morning prayer. To Keith Ulrich for sharing Ignatian consolation and prayer— *requiescat in pace.* I am grateful for International Christian University and its generosity over many decades. My life has been immeasurably better for the fellowship and kindness of many good colleagues at ICU—*omnibus gratias ago.* I am touched by the kindness and sustained friendship over the years of Martin Millar and Martin Murphy. I owe a debt of gratitude to Dan and Felicity Douglas for their hospitable kindness and friendship from Michigan days and to Nobuo and Takako Yoshida in Hiroshima. This book is dedicated to my parents, who taught me to pray and who provided me with an indelible link to Celtic spirituality. I express a debt of gratitude to the Nishizono family for their care and friendship. From childhood I shared a spiritual life with my brother and sisters Adrian, Angela, Christine, Stella, the loved ones who have gone before me: I owe more than I know. The companionship of my wife, Aya, and the joys of my children, Sophie Akane and Julian Kai, are a sine qua non woven into my

Acknowledgements

daily life. The author is responsible for the opinions expressed in this text as well as any errors that may have occurred. All translations from Irish, Japanese, French, and Spanish are by the author.

Preface

The Neighborhood of Souls

SOME PRAYERS ARE DELICATE and profound. They brighten us as we step out, into the sun, from church or synagogue or temple—those neighborhoods of souls. Prayers linger and bend in the mind, like apples on a tree, with a vision of reality, restoring for a moment the eternity we knew as a child. Some prayers are said in haste, full of staccato imperatives, hungering for an answer—Please! Hear me! Now! Prayers are recited with heads bowed, with fingers twined, at dinner, in a house with a roof, or in a refugee tent. An old man falls asleep murmuring a prayer his mother taught him. A woman sits in a chair, shakes her sleeve and tears fall out; she prays in poverty and loneliness. Prayers sit in the mind of a priest or nurse, at a child's bedside, when no more can be done. Ingest the loss and pray. Only prayer can modify brute fact.

Each person has a deep disposition to pray, and each simple prayer is a reinvention of language. Language is the instrument of prayer simply because language is the primary expression, in human life, of who we are and what we are at any moment. Prayer is a creative language art that each person is able to do. Language speaks in a thousand styles and voices. Yet, prayer—like the deep structure of human language itself—issues from an original source. Prayer is a creative capacity of the soul, a transformational grammar that makes it possible for the spirit to sing and speak, to praise, petition, and weep.

This is a book of prayers, with some accompanying comments on the act of praying. These prayers are "scenes from daily life." They touch upon different topics: a prayer for animals, a prayer of the unemployed, a prayer before a river. Whatever prayer we make, it is always sent and always received. Of course, "sending" and "receiving" are uncomfortable metaphors. Prayer is not email. Not yet. Prayer is simpler, and more complex. It is a rapport between heaven and earth, between God and humanity.

1

On Praying

In the Main of Light

WHAT AM I DOING when I pray? Prayers are words, and the silences between words. Words and silence become prayer when we make them so. They are made sacred by us. Heaven touches earth. The spirit of the divine gives itself through language. Prayer is always more than language can contain, more than we (can) say, more like a flooding river.

Praying calls upon an unnamable divine spirit that races through our mortal bodies to tend the immortal being of our souls—to make infinite use of finite means. In religious talk, we say that prayer shines a light in our darkness. In Shakespeare talk, prayer is a little nativity that "puts us in the main of light."[1]

Praying is not meant to last. Prayer moves on. Imagine a hell of continuous prayer. We are in transit. Pray, move on.

French literary theorist Roland Barthes entitled his study of St. Ignatius of Loyola *Comment parler à Dieu?* (How to Speak to God?). Barthes suggested that prayer—an *interlocution divine*, "a divine conversation," is not the search for great or even good words. Rather, when praying we find ourselves in a kind of "linguistic

---

1. Shakespeare, "Sonnet 60."

vacuum" necessary for the "triumph of a new language."[2] We can say that such a vacuum is a space of holding. This squares with the Quaker approach to prayer, which consists of silent waiting—for new language. A Friend may ask the group to "hold someone in the light"—a person who is sick or struggling. In Quaker worship this is more than simple intercessionary prayer, i.e., praying for a person. It is a call by just one little gathering, a society of friends, at one moment in time, to clear the way, to make a road, to hold another, to bear them towards love.

Feelings: Making Space for the Real

You don't want prayer that makes you feel worse. But prayer is not meant to fill us with nice feelings. It does not enfold us in petals. Praying does demand of us deep feeling, or to feel deeply. In fact, praying empties us of emotion, sometimes suddenly. Like emptying a folder stuffed with useless emails that hang out so many emotions—fear, nostalgia, regret, shame. Press. Pray. Delete. Praying off-loads things. It makes space for the holy, the sacred spirit. Praying permits us to "feel" more truly and in a different way. We feel trustful in the divine presence. We are safe because this presence comes to us with no conditions.

The Desire for the Sacred

Praying is a struggle. No, it can get worse than that. It's a beast. As Jean Danielou writes, "to make space for prayer is a battle because prayer is . . . at cross-currents with the habits of the world . . . which gives it less and less space . . . Prayer finds difficulty in securing space."[3]

To pray is a thing of beauty. It is the desire for the sacred. There is liturgy old and new. There are soaring choirs and community hymns, litanies and incantations, prayers with beads,

---

2. Barthes, *Sade, Fourier, Loyola*.
3. Danielou, *Prayer*, 54.

congregational shoulder-to-shoulder prayer, or intimate family devotions; prayer with lit candles and incense, spontaneous prayer, and private silence. There is no single, "certified" method of prayer. It is culturally diverse. Your prayers are just you and the ultimate reality—God. Prayer is a disposition—making yourself open to the divine. Is a fissure in the flux of existence, a pause in the claustrophobia of the self. You make it so. Your prayer is the truth of you.

When we pray we balance forces: an equilibrium of heaven and earth. To stay put in either place is to get stuck, either in life's zigzag or in the self-absorption of religion. This is what Simone Weil called in *Gravity and Grace* "obedience to the power of gravity . . . the greatest sin."[4] Through prayer we accept willingly, with feet on the ground, the gravitational pull of heaven as it comes together, self-delighting and manifesting recognition.

Through the Doors

Each person has an impulse, deep inside, to look for meaning in life. It is an impulse to see through the tossing and turning of everyday life and death. Prayer is a door that leads through and beyond. "Lift up your heads, O gates!And lift them up, O ancient doors" (Ps 24:5). That is why Orthodox religious icons are painted only on doors. These doors, of red, black and gold, bid us enter. Whether you are awake or distracted, content or unhappy, these are the doors to reality. Your prayers are just you.

When we walk—run, scream—through the doors of prayer we may find on other side nothing much at all. It may be a dull place, unfrequented by the sun. A remote darkness, even. Yet, it is darkness that glows. Because this is a sacred place. It is a place of re-creation. On the fourth of day of creation, darkness, together with light, is declared good. Let there be darkness.

Without explanation, this dull place of prayer makes me just a bit more real, more visible to myself than before. The old images—the old me—start to blur. A kind of nativity stirs among the

---

4. Weil, *La Pesanteur et la Grâce*, 27.

silence and words. Something is there, something in there. I am not sure what or who it is. It strives to "lighten our darkness." The Jesuit poet Gerard Manley Hopkins (1844–1889) pointed to a second creation of the sacred darkness in "Christmas Prayer,"

> Moonless darkness stands between.
> Past, the Past, no more be seen!
> But the Bethlehem star may lead me
> To the sight of Him who freed me
> From the self that I have been.

Espresso and Prayer's Erasure

Praying adds time—moments or hours—to our daily life but otherwise subtracts from it. Prayer doesn't rev us up. It isn't an espresso in the morning. In fact, prayer might send us back into the world curiously unsatisfied, unfinished. As though we didn't quite do it properly. This is a good. Erasure is how the divine works. Something was removed inside of us, in order to make room for the divine. We do not fill our soul with prayer. We pray in order to empty our soul. Then we are ready to fill it with the world. God's world—the one I was given to live in. Learning to pray is like when children are taught to dance. They must let go of the body in order to turn into a bird or a tree or the wind. The discipline of prayer shifts our pattern of doing and moving—towards freedom. Then we can become anything. Then, as Thomas Cranmer writes resonantly in the *Book of Common Prayer*, we draw closer to God, "not in bondage of figure or shadow, but in the freedom of the Spirit."[5]

The Hip-Hop of Prayer

The Psalms are a mash-up of beauty and brutality. They are methodology. They teach us how to pray. *Psalm* is from the Greek word *psalmoi*, meaning instrumental music and words. The Psalms express many different things, from praise and thanksgiving

---

5. Cranmer, "Preface," xi.

to dramatic dissatisfaction with how the world is ordered. The Psalms—the longest book of the Bible—are an interesting genre. They show two special qualities: hope and unpredictability. In a slab of psalm we notice a peculiar style: prose and poetry—full of rhythmic messages, delightful turns of phrase, aggressions and contradictions. They teem with poetry, microaggressions, calls for death and divine vengeance on "our enemies," curses, and exquisite tenderness. Mercy! Mercy! The Psalms tell it all. Read the Psalms for what they are. Don't wish for what they are not. Read the Psalms and hear hip-hop.

The Uncertainty of Being Me

Prayer is the language of the precarious. The English word *prayer* is related to the notion of "uncertainty," from medieval Latin *precaria*, "doubt," "danger," "dependence on another." Fear and precariousness are the everyday, raw surface of my life. I might be sick or a precariat or a failure or abused or just unhappy. This human condition is buried deep inside me like a radioactive rock, malign and humming. How can prayer put this right? You know what I mean—me, my problem, the human condition. Well, it can't. Benedictine monk John Chapman offers a paradoxical response to the expectations of prayer, in a letter to a troubled nun. "You don't need to be 'put right' you *are* all right . . . God loves us in our misery, and is bringing to Himself in His own way—not in our way."[6]

The Is-ness and Am-ness of God

We see the precariousness of prayer in our search for "knowledge" of God. By praying I make myself open to a realization that God just is. God's is-ness is revealed in the silence. The silence is named. It is the name which cannot be named, I AM WHO I AM. Can we be quiet enough to listen to that namelessness? The identity of God is everywhere and inexhaustible. Listening is a subtle linguistic

---

6. Chapman, Selected Letters, 76.

act. If nothing else, it makes us conscious of an interlocutor. The presence of this listening interlocuter is its own reward. Rowan Williams poignantly remarks, "Because God is God and nothing stops God from being God this ought to generate in us a stillness."[7]

Walls of Change

> I used to pass an old geezer standing at the walls of St Giles. Same place, every day. I once stopped and asked him, "How long have you been doing this, Jimmy?" "Fifty years" he said. "What do you pray for?" "I pray to Almighty God for peace in the world, freedom from injustice, freedom from hatred and poverty." "How's it going?" I asked. He said, "Feels like I'm talking to a wall."
> —Comedian, St Giles Cathedral, Edinburgh Fringe Festival, 2005

To pray is to change something but maybe not some things. Can it change the world? Look for it but don't expect it. And that is not the purpose of prayer anyway. Prayer itself is subject to change. The same prayer feels different the next time we repeat it. Praying changes us. A thought changes. And by the time I return next day, to the same prayer, the praying is different. That's because we are different. Another day in the life. Our mood has changed. We see the same things, but differently.

Common Worship

The church does not sort and categorize us. We face one way: together. Worship in one place at one time demonstrates our shared humanity. The crunching categories that we deal with in daily life disappear—race, ethnicity, minority, and mainstream, cultural and cross-cultural complexity—as we stand together, for a few moments, shoulder to shoulder. There is equality in prayer in

---

7. Williams, "Problem of Prayer.

common. There is liberation. It is the prayer of vulnerable humanity, the prayer of wholeness.

Common worship is regulatory. Like the ringing of bells, common worship keeps you on track. It is a structure. A prayer for this and that and consonant with the seasons of the year—in the Christian faith Advent, Christmas, Lent, Easter—and prayers at Baptism and Marriage and Death. Set liturgical prayer intends to communicate the faith. It shows what faith means. Though solemn and sometimes long, the liturgy is a sensory and intellectual and aesthetic expression of joy.

A Place Made Sacred by Us

Inside the gates, prayer reveals something that was there before, just yesterday—no wait, last year—no wait, a billion years ago. It reveals the mind of God. Prayer is microwave theology. It serves up immediate and profound truth about the nature of God.

Prayer does not put the world at your feet. It cannot make bread from stones. Rather, it makes life available by making a space—ready and receptive. To pray is to allow the divine to enter this cleared space—a divine plenitude. The French word *disponibilité* captures this readiness. *Disponibilité* is having a "receptive" state of the spirit—*état d'esprit*. Prayer is a positioning towards the divine. Sometimes I am conscious of being receptive: in the quiet of a church, walking along the street, sitting in a garden, riding the train.

The divine space within us contains all of our being, as well as the being of others, present and past. It is death that teaches us about this sacred space. In Seamus Heaney's *Clearances*, the Irish poet writes seven poems about the death of his mother. In the elegiac Sonnet VII he sits with the family, all gathered round her bedside. He remembers the ordinary things: folding the washing together, peeling potatoes, sitting in the kitchen, or smelling the candle smoke in a church during Holy Week. He watches in silence at the bedside. Then she dies. When his mother is gone, the space that she once occupied is now the space that "we" occupy—to keep. His mother has made a clearance. A clearance for others. A place has been prepared. An emptying. The tomb was full. No. Now it's empty. There is space to walk, to run. The poet runs like two women at the tomb of Jesus. He runs. They run. In joy and fear. Why inexplicable joy and fear? The lid on this mortal life has been lifted. And Heaney thus writes, "pure change happened."

Turning and Turning Up

In praying, I am transformed in God's way not mine. After all, what I really want is not God. I want a Genie. In a bottle. To wish away my sorrow. Genie, my friend, can you manage a few more wishes? But prayer is not the fulfillment of a wish. It's something different. It's a stance we take, a turning towards. "Then I turned my face to the Lord God, seeking him by prayer and pleas for mercy" (Dan 9:3). Like when the wind changes direction. I set my face, like sails on a boat, willingly or reluctantly, toward God.

We are for turning. It is not necessary to think or speak. Turning. In prayer I put myself somewhere else. It's changing places. Like when I cross a street to walk in the sunshine. We are for turning. What is this place of prayer? What do we find? We enter upon a very large space—a divine place—made sacred, by ourselves. The space is made sacred because we have arrived there. Prayer is us. Prayer is turning up.

To pray is to "turn up." It is our decision to be really present. We turn up because we are tempted—often desperately—to escape; even from those who love us. We want to walk away, from church or synagogue or temple. Kick it. God is not around anyhow. Let me outta here. Perhaps God never was. But God was not absent. God turned up. To pray is about us: turning up. God is there all the time because God is time. We can never be early or late. Each person is in time and a fragment of divine time.

On Praying

The Speech Act

Blessing, thanking, asking, wishing, commenting, praising, interpreting. Prayer is a collection of different acts that do different things. It is because prayers have different purposes that they employ guiding symbols. Twilight is the image in the memorable Sarum Compline from the Middle Ages, translated in a *collect* from the *Book of Common Prayer* (1559). This oration is a prayer of silky style recited, appropriately, at Anglican Evensong: "Lighten our darkness, we beseech thee, O Lord; and by thy great mercy defend us from all perils and dangers of this night; for the love of thy only Son, our Saviour Jesus Christ. Amen." It sounds nice in Latin too: *Illumina, quaesumus, Domine, tenebras nostras: et totius huius noctis insidias tu a nobis repelle propitius.*[8]

This little Tudor prayer inches forward, word by sombre word, carrying us through the hammering darkness of our day and night to a place of serenity. It is the motion of the soul itself.

Prayer is the desire for God. It is expressed as a word or a murmur, even a fleeting thought. Prayer is actual desire; a speech act, a thought act, a physical act. It makes something happen—even if you cannot see it, even if you cannot touch it or feel it or hear it. "But when you pray, go into your room and shut the door and pray to your Father who is in secret. And your Father who sees in secret will reward you" (Matt 6:6).

Say the word. What happens? The doors open. We say the word or think the thought. They open. You can hear something. It's doors creaking.

The Power of Bad Prayer

Never underestimate the power of bad prayer. We prayer for power over others. We violate the bodies and minds of women and men—in God's name. We pray for concrete answers to problems. "Hey Dude! Now!" We lie to God, with lies about ourselves, because we lie to ourselves. Praying is a delaying tactic: instead of

---

8. Frere, *New History*.

making a decision to be better, to do better. We pray as we arm up on the battlefield, for somebody else's war, for death and damage to persons we have never met. We pray for people in our religion but not for "others," "them," in theirs. This is unseemly and sad. We don't see the contradiction. We pray for success in a political campaign, for an ideology, for nationalist goals—our great nation above other nations. We pray for change in things but not change in ourselves. To pray is to be tranquil and compassionate, to turn myself into an obedient listener.

Searching the Face of the Other

The French philosopher Gabriel Marcel in the *Mystery of Being* (1950) reminds us that prayer has two characteristics. Firstly, prayer searches the face of the other because the other is a transcendent mystery. It looks for "good news" from life, from God, from another person. Of course. What else do we expect? Secondly, prayer is "self-centered." It's about us. So what's new? That's who we are. God trades with what we have; not what we don't have. God looks at who we are; not who we are not.

Sure, prayer is self-centered. It is a call for attention, help even. It starts that way and maybe ends that way. And that's OK too because what we deeply desire in prayer will shine through the fog of the request *de jour*. Over time, something else starts to happen—on its own. Prayer, mysteriously, like a speck of yeast, starts to change the shape of the thing we put into it. The more we pray, the more our attention shifts away from "me." Our empathy for other things and others grows. Prayer leads us out of the sandpit of the self, up and out towards a sense of astonished being. Now prayer seems incomplete without the presence of the Other.

2

Prayers

Prayer before a River: Continuity Is Strength

GOD OF HEAVEN AND earth. This river runs through woods and towns and villages. Where does it start? The waters run forward with a purpose, not pausing, not stopping to think too much. I know the river's goal. The river knows it when it stops being a river.

> He is like a tree planted by streams of water that yields its fruit in its season, and its leaf does not wither. In all that he does, he prospers. (Ps 1:3)

A river is living water. It cleanses. It refreshes. Giant rivers run through cities. They flow without complaining. Forward, never backward. Continuity is strength. In one place, the waters are a fast torrent, in another place they meander. A river connects people. A river does its job: carrying stones and plants and fish and people. It never surrenders.

God of heaven and earth. A river is what I want to be. The river holds our spiritual world. Holy people have gone to rivers seeking wisdom. Rivers give nourishment. I seek them out. They give quiet and calm.

> When you pass through the waters, I will be with you;
> and through the rivers, they shall not overwhelm you.
> (Isa 43:2)

The river is like You and me. Watching the river, I can slip into the world that waits for me. Your world. Wait for me down by the river.

God of strength and peace You restore my soul.

Prayer of the Bereaved: Into the Main of Light

Almighty God. This death has changed me. The death of my waking hours, my sleep. This monstrous pain. Death has become a way of life.

The soul of my loved one is now with You. You can have it. I just want her body. Now. Nothing will comfort me. I just want that body back. Here. Death is absurd. The hurt and the grief. I get up and go out and work. I know it must go on. Speaking to You is consolation. I know I am not alone. I am just one of many mourners on this day, in this town, on this earth. I will tell others what my loved one was like. They will listen. People are good.

> The Lord is close to the broken-hearted and saves those
> who are crushed in spirit. (Ps 34:18)

Almighty God. My grief is important to You. I know why. That is the purpose of death. To remind us we do not fit perfectly into life. Perfection is death.

Death stopped me in my tracks. I walked into a wall. It makes me quiet. It makes my soul tremble. No, more than that. It makes me know my soul. The goodness of death.

My grief has its own timetable. Unexpected emotions rise and fall. Take death with a good heart.

> For everything there is a season, and a time for every
> matter under heaven: a time to be born, and a time to die
> (Eccl 3:1–8)

Prayers

Talking to You I am already beyond space and time. I am already beyond death. You dare me, "Go on then! Affirm both life and death!" Almighty God. Without death the doors of heaven are shut. Life and death are woven together. Without life death makes no sense. Without death life makes no sense.
    We must make this journey. Without death we cannot live. With death the gates to eternity open. Almighty God. My sorrow is not despair. Sorrow is sacred. It is like happiness. This death has told me, once and for all, that I am not the centre of life.

Prayer of the Insomniac: Fixing the Noise in My Life

Almighty God. The zigzag in my life is almost too much to bear. It's a noise in my head. It keeps me awake. I can't leave it behind. Things, people, money, sickness, work. I go to bed dragging a whole city behind me.
    I hear the silence of the night. You know that this noise, this sleeplessness, is real life. My problem has its own greatness. It's my life. It is what You will for us. Everything mixed up. Quiet, noise. Going forward, going backward. I accept it. This is what You want.

> Come to me all you who are weary and burdened and I will give you rest. (Matt 17:28)

    Yes. You know what I really want. That's for sure. You give me only what You will. Enough to see me through the day. Thy will be done. In the meantime I can do something. You know, sleep hygiene, sleep techniques. It's out there. It need it. I won't play the hero. I'll fix it.
    I will turn to You. Even without thinking of You. In the noise of the night. In my sleeplessness. In the noise of my day.

> I lay down and slept; I woke again, for the Lord sustained me. (Ps 3:5, NIV)

God of strength and peace You restore my soul.

Prayer for the Animals: God's Loved Creatures

Almighty God. The creatures of this world are full of God. They have the breath of life. They are creatures of the same divine origin as us. They were made by You. They have feeling. They play and suffer. They are part of the grand plan of life. These mortals are our companions. We share the same earth.

> For what happens to the children of man and what happens to the beasts is the same; as one dies, so dies the other. They all have the same breath, and man has no advantage over the beasts, for all is vanity. (Eccl 3:19, NIV)

My fellow creatures have a right to the fulfillment of their lives. They are not living things of no importance. They are creatures of value. Yet we hunt and trade and torture them. We spoil and enslave them. We buy and abandon them like commodities. Let us value them, not for what they can do for us, but for what they are. Let us show generosity to animals. Does it help to think sometimes of an animal as she and he not it?

> But ask the beasts, and they will teach you;
> the birds of the heavens, and they will tell you;
> or the bushes of the earth, and they will teach you;
> and the fish of the sea will declare to you.
> (Job 12:7–8, NIV)

Almighty God. Teach us to be a good shepherd like You. Let us draw animals into our circle of compassion. To respect them as fellow mortals. To value their lives as their own. Help us heal the enmity that exists between people and animals.

> And to every beast of the earth and to every bird of the heavens and to everything that creeps on the earth, everything that has the breath of life. (Gen 1:30)

The animals are not separate from us. We are part of the animal kingdom. Teach me that the mercy I show Your creatures is the measure of my mercy toward persons. Then I can live in peace with the rest of creation.

God of strength and peace You restore my soul.

Prayers

Prayer of a Sick Person: Reviewing Life

Almighty God. I am anxious. Frightened. Will I get better? Maybe. Maybe not. I'm ill. Why me? What did I do wrong? My body is broken. This illness robs me of optimism.

No, I don't need optimism. Give me faith, instead. That is where the power lies. People, friends, relatives, colleagues look out for me. Some are looking after me. There is medication. It can help. Nurses and doctors listen to my silence. Oh! Humanity! I am grateful!

> Fear not, for I am with you;
> do not be dismayed, for I am your God.
> I will strengthen you I will help you. (Isa 41:10)

Now that I am suffering I can see other people suffering in different ways. Damaged in body, and mind, suffering terror, loss of faith, despair in personal relation. It's funny, suddenly my own illness has opened my eyes and removed my fear of many other things.

> Heal me, O Lord, and I shall be healed; save me and I shall be saved, for you are my praise. (Jer 17:14)

My sickness makes me ask questions. Am I a nuisance to other people? Do I fail to express my gratitude to carers? You ask for my acceptance of the world. You want my trust in You.

> The Lord sustains him on his sickbed; in his illness you restore him to full health. (Ps 41:3)

Turning to You, Eternal God, the chaos stops. I can go on. During this sickness I will review my life. I am not inferior because of illness. Life has a purpose. This is how it is. I must go on. Get me back on my feet. I still have the power to make changes—however small—in my life. I will keep positive when I feel negative. I will seek out one moment of inner peace rather than a day of melancholy. Trust in God gives inner peace.

God of strength and peace You restore my soul.

Prayer of a Parent: Loving with a Broken Heart

Eternal God. I am a parent. I like children—other people's. Maybe not my child. Their behavior offends me. It's like my loving child's place has been taken over by someone else whose headed for self-destruction. It's like every day this child is a sword that runs me through. Get out of my sight kid. Just go. Or maybe I should go. I know these solutions won't work.

Almighty God. This is not the child I expected. It's the child I have. But I will try not to confuse their behavior with the person standing before me. We do not love personality; we love a person.

I will seek moments of prayer and rest. I will seek help. From a counselor. From wise friends. I will go on talking in a civil and kindly manner. I will avoid humiliating my child, keep showing interest, show different perspectives and explain my negative responses. I know. Raising children is a "sacrifice." That means I am in a sacred undertaking. Sacred sacrifice? In Latin, *sacer*, "holy," and *facere*, "to make." You're kidding. No. My sacrifice is the cultivation of holiness. Children can heal the spirit.

> I will strengthen you, I will help you,
> I will uphold you with my righteous right hand.
> (Isa 41:10)

I believe that my children too will one day turn water into wine. They too, one day, will delight me. This belief gives me hope and hope is God's shadow on earth.

> Let your father and mother be glad; let her who bore you rejoice.
> (Prov 23:25)

There's "stuff" I cannot fix. Them. Me. I am fearful. I'm a coward. I know that. It's worse. They know that. But they need me around. Parents are a sounding board. To hear not command. To set example not run down. To empathize not expel.

Holy Spirit give me the wisdom to think straight, to keep communication with my children. Things will change. I will survive this grief. It will go away. I will not go away. I must love with a broken heart.

God of strength and peace You restore my soul.

Prayer of a Worker: Building Creation

Almighty God. My work is my livelihood. It's a necessity. There is satisfaction in doing a good job. Work matters. I can serve my fellow human beings. Honorable work makes the monotony bearable. Honorable work is holy.

> I know that there is nothing better for people than to be happy and to do good while they live. That each of them may eat and drink, and find satisfaction in all their toil—this is the gift of God. (Eccl 3:12–13)

Adam and Eve were gardeners. These employees got distracted and fired. My work doesn't run smooth either. I often go in circles. There is daily anxiety. Monotony. I put up with nastiness, and incompetence—mine included. There are good times and bad times. What do I expect? But it can get much worse. Working life is sometimes stained by injustice, sometimes exploitation. Then it's not work but slavery. That is an insult to Your holy purpose.

My faith has a good influence on my work morality. Almighty God. You give us abilities. They're not ready-made. I must learn how to use them and improve them. God set humanity to live and work on the earth. When I work I help to build a decent world, Your creation.

Almighty God. The bad in work is easily understood. How can I grasp the good? I want to see the good. The privilege of work. The joy in work. Joy is free of charge. Work provides us with friends, with colleagues and mentors.

> Behold, what I have seen to be good and fitting is to eat and drink and find enjoyment in all the toil with which one toils under the sun the few days of his life that God has given him, for this is his lot. (Eccl 5:18)

God of strength and peace You restore my soul.

Prayer of an Agnostic:
God Means Nothing, and Something

Almighty God. I'll keep this short. When humanity asked who you are you were reluctant to be named.

> I AM WHO I AM. (Exod 3:14)

Neither will I challenge your identity. You are the Unnamable God. I recognize that. I am one of your people. One who will not and cannot name you. I thank you for giving me a special place on your mountain.

You know how it is about religion, about faith. You're in and you're out at the same time. I mean, there is part of me that wants in. I think I'm happy to be outside. I don't know.

The idea of God is a burden. I understand the idea but I am not . . . what shall I say? Persuaded? I am where I am. On the periphery. Is it lack of will? Is it a lack of humility? Maybe I know better. Or maybe I don't know better. I don't know.

Religion is in the way. I'm in the way.

There are too many issues with religion: terrible believers and their terrible beliefs, unkind rules, know-all pastors, rock star pastors, religious excuses for all manner of murder, cruelty and discrimination. It goes on and on. Don't get me started. Did I say I'd keep this short?

I ignore the wonderful works of churches and religious people who work for the poor and the downtrodden. They work in Your presence as they toil in schools and neighborhoods, in prisons and hospitals and refugee camps. I'm a bystander.

> Make me to know your ways, O Lord; teach me your paths.
> (Ps 25:4)

This prayer might be a waste of time. What are you doing here anyway? You are the hidden God, hidden inside me. I want to worship you but I'm not sure. I know that my unbelief does not take you away. I might be just an ignorant jerk. I think I seek you earnestly. I want to pray. But maybe not to you. I just want to pray. Is it that same thing? I don't know.

My conversation with you was not short. Maybe that means something.

I realize that each time I pray silently—sitting on a park bench, contemplating a tree—I am in the presence of God. It teaches me something. Prayer makes me a channel for the world of Spirit. It opens me up. This is a channel for you and the world I live in. Let it come.

God of strength and peace you restore my soul.

Prayer of a Person in Love: Actually

Eternal God. It's the real thing. That's what I say. Things are shaken up. My world looks different. What's going on? It's love, actually. Love has taught me something strange: that there's a source of love. The source is real. The wellspring affirms me. It's in me. It's in the person I love.

This love seems even to change things around me. I think I'll name it "transubstantiation." I mean, my body and soul have changed. This love seems even to make dead things come alive.

Almighty God, it's said that You created the thing called "love"; I don't know why You did this but I give thanks. A church billboard proclaims, "God is love." I can't always work that out. But I know that in this new love my days are deeper and bigger. It's an openness to life. This love unites things inside that were disconnected. It heals some of the brokenness. It even seems to be the meaning of life. God is love? Maybe I get it.

> Set me as a seal upon your heart, as a seal upon your arm,
> for love is strong as death, jealousy is fierce as the grave.
> Its flashes are flashes of fire, the very flame of the Lord.
> Many waters cannot quench love, neither can floods drown it.
> (Song 8:6–7)

I will keep watch over this love as You will watch over me.
God of strength and peace You restore my soul.

Prayer for No More War: Wisdom Is Compassion

It's permanent night. A sordid world. Bombs, rockets, warships, drones, guns. Oh! The horror! In the good name of justice, laying waste to towns and neighborhoods and fields. The jeopardized bodies. The blighted lives. And they prepare for more.

Darkness to darkness. And there You are, Almighty God, in the middle of the dark, at its desolate center.

> They have blown the trumpet and made everything ready, but no one is going to the battle, for My wrath is against all their multitude. (Ezek 7:14)

We think we are wise but the most perfect wisdom is compassion. To become one with other people. Compassion is the essential matter.

> In that day I will also make a covenant for them With the beasts of the field, The birds of the sky And the creeping things of the ground And I will abolish the bow, the sword and war from the land, And will make them lie down in safety. (Hos 2:18)

Almighty God. Help us question our comfortable distinctions like "friend and enemy," "good and evil," "black and white." I will show compassion to all who grieve amidst the chaos of war, and because of violence done to them. I will show compassion for those who mourn the dead, those who weep for the wounded in body and spirit.

God of strength and peace You restore my soul.

Prayer for Friendship: Lies, Strength, Trust

Friendship is wonderful. Friends strengthen me. Friends give affection and support. In good times and bad times. We trade secrets. Do big talk and small talk.

Good friends will conceal from you and lie. I know. They are concerned for you. They look out for you. I give thanks for my friends even when they're wrong. Good friends will tell you the truth. They care for you. I must listen to them humbly. Friends communicate with each other; tough things they need to hear.

> Iron sharpens iron and one man sharpens another.
> (Prov 27:17)

Friendship, Aristotle wrote, is "a single soul dwelling in two bodies." There is trust. I know my friend won't go out especially to hurt me or poison me.

Almighty God. Friendship is like my connection to You. Friendship does not mean I like my friends all the time. I don't see eye to eye with some friends. So what. Friendship is our bond. I trust my friend. They do not play games with me.

Almighty God. I trust You. Knowing You is important. Friendship is trust. Our connection is true and strong and mysterious.

> Oil and perfume make the heart glad, and the sweetness of a friend comes from his earnest counsel. (Prov 27:9)

God of strength and peace You restore my soul.

Prayer of an Unrepentant Sinner: Honor Your Imperfections

Almighty God. I am sorry for my sins. I do not feel sorry for all of them. Some of them. Sometimes sorrowfully, when I think about it.

I will sin again. I have a list. It's circular. Like making promises to myself. When it comes to breaking them I'm Your man. I'm half-hearted. I'm a scoundrel. I will sin again. Yes, that one, especially that one. But I will not despair. Regression is part of progress. Despair is for losers.

You ask only for my humility and my desire for holiness. You have it. For You this desire is growth. I am growing in grace. You know that I think about myself too much: what I should feel and not feel. You shake Your head and counsel me to stop fretting about "my spiritual life." You tell me that wringing my hands is a waste of precious time—"Just get on with it. Get on with doing better." Got it.

I will be less ambitious, more simple. I will not beat myself up. Temptation and sin have a disciplinary value. I will honor my imperfections.

Everything that happens to me—thinking, doing—is the hand of God. I'm OK. Give me awareness of the bad things I do. Give me sympathy for the victims of my sin.

> Have mercy on me, O God, according to your steadfast love; according to your abundant mercy. (Ps 51:1)

Every little thing is a ladder to heaven. Every moment is a step to heaven. Stay with me.

God of strength and peace You restore my soul.

Prayer before a Christmas Tree: The Dignity of Nature

Almighty God. We brought You home. You stand in our house. Welcome. While the rest of nature sleeps, you are evergreen and watchful. Throughout the day. On Christmas night. Our Christmas tree is sign of the faithfulness of God that persists, that never fades.

In Your strength I see a path through winter, the determination of the magi on long roads, the constancy of angels who sing in a dark sky. This tree points to spring and better times, evergreen in the midst of winter, strong in the wind and cold.

Almighty God, the history of our salvation begins with a tree and ends with a tree.

Almighty God. Evergreen in winter, let me sleep on Christmas night, beneath the stars of this tree, and wake on Christmas morning, to the brightness of its branches.

Let me arise on Christmas morning and stand with the dignity of a tree, like a new person born a second time, forgiven, forgiving and strong.

> Then shall the trees of the forest sing for joy.
> (1 Chr 16:33)

God of strength and peace You restore my soul.

Morning Prayer

God of heaven and earth. Morning light. Another biodegradable day. The days come in. They go out. God is my constant.

> God is in the midst of her; she shall not be moved;
> God will help her when morning dawns. (Ps 46:5)

Accompany me through this day. Take my hand on the road. I don't feel too good. Put my head back on my shoulders. Bring on the day.

Let me value this world and my earth-born companions who share it. Those that I live and work with. Today, I will take one minute to close my eyes and be quiet. Today I will not beat myself up. I will have a kind thought and word for myself and for the persons who are a pain in my life.

Today, with a good heart, I will listen to other people, give them a little space. You know I'm an inflexible person. I don't change my mind easily. It's a sad thing. Can I forgive someone today?

When I walk down the street I will look at the things in Your creation. It's a long list. The sky, the road ahead, plants and trees, technology, buildings where people live, art, music and conversations. I know that through the appearance of these things God appears to me.

> My voice You shall hear in the morning, O LORD; In
> the morning I will direct it to You, And I will look up.
> (Ps 5:3)

I will look up because there, in the clouds, You are. I will look down. Because there, on the road, You are. Eternal God, God of heaven and earth, give me strength for the day and guide me along the right way.

God of strength and peace You restore my soul.

Night Prayer

God of heaven and earth. The end of another day. The silence and the darkness. I'm grateful for sleep. The peace of sleep.

> In peace I will both lie down and sleep; for you alone, O Lord, make me dwell in safety. (Ps 4:8)

Today I did some things right. I made a mess of other things. I don't think too much about it. I'm superficial. Did I wrong someone today? I will try to make amends. Perhaps apologize. Did I lose control in pointless anger, greed? I will hold things together tomorrow. What are the seven deadly sins and the opposite virtues? I need to look them up. I need to sleep.

> For he will command his angels concerning you to guard you in all your ways. (Ps 91:11)

Watch over me this night, spirits of the dead that love me. Guardian angel from heaven so bright, watch over me this starry night.

> Return, O my soul, to your rest; for the Lord has dealt bountifully with you. (Ps 116:7)

Eternal God. It is a consolation that someone really knows me. You know all that I am. I do not worry what will happen tomorrow. Let it happen. In every struggle You watch over me.

God of strength and peace You restore my soul.

Prayer of the Faiths: Border Work

Almighty God, the religions of the world are godsends. Their plurality is God's grace to us. They are God inspired, Your plan, experiments in love and truth. They proclaim Your action in the world, revelations of You.

I sometimes wish people would be more like me and my religion. But I know that is not possible or wise. We all need to work harder. Our religions must change and grow. We all need to do some border-work.

Religions live in a hubbub of people and languages, cultures and histories. Where else would they be? Some religious practices don't seem just to all its men and women. I'll start with my own religion. It's not comfortable. The path forward is affirmation and renewal.

Where there is uniformity let us sow community. Where there is monologue let us make dialogue. To imagine a vision of unity is to make a vision for humanity. Through dis-course we see our different directions. Through con-course we walk forward in reflection. Only then can religions be themselves.

Faith is a movement of the heart that opens towards God. It is an inner virtue. Alone we cannot know everything about the virtuous life. Learning from each other in different places and time, we strive to be human in the shelter of the Divine.

God of strength and peace You restore my soul.

Prayer of a Texter: AG Can We Text?

almighty god can we text?
reaching out to U
can i get your mail address?
Instagram Twitter Facebook and LINE
R YOU ok?
(*^‿^*)
they help us CONNECT!
my phone is good i plan i chat . . . information on the go
it keeps my time.. helps me work . . . i'm in the flow
idk if it's just me
talking's good but it's not efficient
talk's face-to-face and my face is deficient
we can text . . . do stuff AT THE SAME TIME!
in the bathroom . . . waiting in line
i got a problem can't disconnect
we sleep together omg
it's a MESS!
csws

Prayers Before a River

my routine's a wreck
(-_-)
almighty god can i text U
i'm on the screen right now i'm home
i know you're everywhere . . . inside my phone.
lol
almighty god get me outta here.. reaching out to U
i have a problem don't know what to do
i get anxious when my battery's low . . .
i can't cut back but i'm NOT a complete FOOL!
i'm glad i can talk to U
i'll plan my day
make phone-free time ok
phone-free zones.. bathroom bedroom
disable stuff that's sending my life away
almighty god can i talk to U?
i'll dump the apps that hook me, stuff with no purpose
I will not set before my eyes anything that is worthless psalm 101:3
Hey! RAISE my day's EXPECTATIONS!
turn off notifications
i'll put it away . . . it'll be a shock
almighty god please TAKE ME AS I AM!
and . . . can I borrow your alarm clock?
lol
bbl

gspUrms

3

On Praying

Prayer as the Making of Meaning

RITUALS HELP SHAPE OUR human experience of life. They contain the potency of order. Think of the days of the week. What you do on Monday morning compared to Friday night and Sunday afternoon. Think of the way you make tea and dress and greet people. Rituals establish order and thereby help us take control. Prayer as ritual is, therefore, not the communication of meaning but the creation of meaning. It is a creative force. A prayer in the morning recognizes a new day; family prayer before eating respectfully opens a meal. These are condensed symbols that express solidarity with the living and the dead.

The ritual of praying is a reconciliation of life's contradictions. Prayer inserts into the dimensions of nature transcendent purpose. The anthropologist Mary Douglas in *Purity and Danger* (1966) argued that believers in the Judeo-Christian world of the Middle Ages did not expect liturgical rituals to serve up instant solutions to problems. Rather, rituals and ritual prayers opened up a path to the miraculous. Douglas suggested we consider sacred ritual and ritual prayer not in terms of magic but miracles. Prayer opens up the radical possibility of a unity in our existence. It renders the possibility that the unexpected can indeed happen.

Time's Things

Prayer works quietly and effectively through gaps in life. To make space for prayer is to make an interval or opening in the middle of the solid wall of things around us. With effort we squeeze through a gap in the wall like children at play. The core structure of this gratitude and attention.

Shinto, "the way of the deities," is the folk religion of Japan. It has no scripture or single founder and, superficially, is the reverse of belief in one God. Its single ethical injunction is "gratitude" to the divine. Each thing in the world is imbued with *kami* or "spirit": the wind, a tree, the ground, and ancestors. They respond to human prayer. They are spiritualized things. Likewise, the qualities that things possess, such as beauty and strangeness and fear, are expressions of a sacred spirit. *Kami* are not perfect. They are not in themselves "God." In the Shinto view of life simple objects become divine after one hundred years; like the big brown wooden door of my school in Scotland, the cooking pot my mother left me, the leather bag my grandfather gave me, a woolen shawl my aunt made for my child. Objects attain dignity with use. We are grateful to them because they support us. Gratitude make us happy and concerned for things around us. In Japan, soccer supporters tidy their stadium after a football match, people sweep footpaths near their house, children in elementary public schools tidy their own classrooms, serve school lunch to others and clean the floors of their school.

Organizing consultant Marie Kondo wrote an influential book titled *The Life-Changing Magic of Tidying Up: The Japanese Art of Decluttering and Organizing* (2014). We imagine Ms. Kondo sitting quietly on the floor of her house. She thanks her home, she taps some books, wakes up her clothes. It takes imagination. It is the shape gratitude takes. You greet the morning, kettle and mugs. To objects being tossed out you thank them, for giving you pleasure. To your old pair of shoes you thank them for sharing their life. Mockery comes easy in such a scenario, but wait a moment. What's going on here? For Kondo, a former Shinto shrine attendant maiden, this is a form of compassion. It is an acknowledgement of my relation to things. A religious view of the world means that things lose their simple utilitarian objectivity. Don't know Shinto? It's a religion. Look it up.

Objects deserve veneration. This is difficult to do in the "amassing society." They have a divine life. The everyday philosophy of declutter is based on gratitude. Only when we have gratitude are we free to move on with life. Gratitude for today and yesterday—not an easy game to play. Yet, gratitude is the beginning and end of our relation to other persons.

Discover the holiness of time and time's things. Slow down. When we do things deliberately, when we eat a bit more slowly, when we savor a cup of coffee, walk deliberately. Bathing and exercising, cleaning and cooking, studying, washing my cup and saucer, sharpening a pencil.

We are often urged to "set aside time" for prayer. This is a curious turn of phrase.

Giving attention to prayer means that we try to do things one at a time. It is a "waiting," the attention of the waiting soul. It takes effort.

Prayers and Books

The twelfth-century philosopher and rabbi Maimonides in the *Mishneh Torah*, "Laws of Prayer," noted that until the Babylonian exile (586 BCE) the Jewish faithful composed their own prayers, that is, until the composition of the *Siddur*, the Jewish prayer book which established an order of daily prayers.[1] Having a prayer routine is a way to organize your life—reciting a morning prayer, a prayer before meals. A prayer routine gives order; *siddur* is the Hebrew word for, you guessed it, "order" or "arrangement."

Liturgical prayer is called "worship." It involves the whole person. There is smell: the characteristic smell of your church, candle wax and incense. There is action: bowing, kneeling, standing,

---

1. Birnbaum, *Maimonides' Code of Law and Ethics*.

making the sign of the cross, and raising our hands. There is sight: a physical church, vestments, an altar, a procession, an icon. There is taste: bread and wine in the Eucharist. There is sound: reciting, singing, chanting, and the sound of bells. Divine worship is usually named the "Liturgy of Saint John Chrysostom" or the "Liturgy of Saint Basil the Great" in the Orthodox Church.

An influential prayer book emerged in the English Reformation, *The Book of Common Prayer* (1549/1552/1662). These liturgical prayers, under editor Thomas Cranmer, the archbishop of Canterbury, are used in the worldwide Anglican Communion. Lutheran, Methodist and Presbyterian forms of worship also borrow from this compilation. Some prayer is ecumenical, like the Taizé formula founded in 1940 in the small French town of Taizé. Christians of all traditions use music, readings and silent reflection.

Great prayers have been composed in many languages and times. The Psalms of the Hebrew Bible—Christianity's Old Testament—are prayerful laments and praises of unknown authorship. The Lord's Prayer uttered by Jesus (Matt 6:9–13) is probably most famous prayer in the world.

Many stand-alone prayers are well known, like "The Prayer of St Patrick" of Ireland, St. Francis of Assisi's "Instrument of Your Peace." In the twentieth century there are widely circulated prayers like Thomas Merton's "Lead Me" or "The Serenity Prayer" of Reinhold Niebuhr. There are prayer collections in the English language tradition, like the Benedictine Augustine Baker's compilation in the midst of a bubonic plague in sixteenth-century London and prayers of his contemporary Anglican cleric Jeremy Taylor, "the Shakespeare of the divines."

Having an Attitude

Prayer is an attitude. It means putting yourself in a prayerful state of mind—whether you say anything or not. In fact, prayer is not what you say but the shape of how you say it.

To pray is take up a dis-position, different from usual. After all, when we have conversation with someone we turn to look at

On Praying

them. Likewise, when we turn out to pray we turn out our spirit. Inside the space of prayer we settle into a new position. We put our hands together, sit, bow our heads or kneel. Religion puts us in the disposition of prayer. The room itself is space made sacred by us. Christians have kneelers, Buddhist temples have cushions, and Muslims have prayer rugs.

In some religions prayer involves prostration. Face on the ground. For Muslim faithful there is standing and bowing and prostrating, which is the deepest expression of humility, submission and helplessness—to "prostrate and draw near" to God. And in which direction do you kneel? When Muhammad was wondering whether he should be praying towards Jerusalem or toward the Ka'ba in Mecca, something was revealed to him on the solidarity of prayer in all religions. Namely, that people face in their own way in their own direction but wherever they are God brings them all together.[2] Prostration of the body is an expression of humility. Metropolitan Archbishop Anthony Bloom in *Beginning to Pray* reminds us that "humility" derives from the Latin word *humus*, meaning "soil," "loam," the rich organic component of soil. Strong-smelling earth is in a field, in a garden, in a park. Always in the open, it receives rain, wind and sunshine. It is open to the change of the seasons. It is open to new possibilities, ready to receive the seed we sow, capable of bringing forth. The ground is what we walk on. Start with humility, then prayer can begin. Probably on the ground. Maybe on our knees.

Ticktock, Ticktock, Ticktock

Distraction reminds us of where we are. Prayer increases our awareness of the world around. Once upon a time, R. Dov Baer of Lubavitch was at prayer in his room. His daughter was in a cradle. She fell out onto the floor and started wailing. Her father, deep in prayer, heard nothing. His father, R. Schneur Zalman, heard the noise and rushed into the room. Returning the baby to its cradle,

---

2. Nasr et al., *Study Quran*, 2:148.

he scolded his son, "Isn't there any room in your head for anything else? When I am in prayer I can hear the sound of a fly crawling up the window pane!"[3] The ticking clock, voices in the street, a police siren. A distraction is not a site of battle. Acknowledge the distraction politely, gratefully (you are alive!), then let it go and you go back to what you were doing.

We need not be anxious about distraction, about prayer. Did you ever say the same prayer twice or three times because, irritatingly, you "didn't say it properly" the first time? That way lies madness. Or maybe not. Perhaps it is sweet and gentle to say a prayer twice in succession, fast and slow. Perfect prayer? You will never get it right because there isn't one. We do what we can. In all we do. Among Martin Buber's Hasidic sayings, he tells of the rabbi of Kotzk who called out his students who were talking about the need for "earnestness" in prayer.

> "What is all this blabber about praying earnestly?!
> What does it mean, to 'pray earnestly?!'"
> They did not understand him.
> "Is there anything at all that one may do without earnestness?" he said.[4]

The Symbolic Language of Prayer

The one who prays must not be troubled by the inadequate language of prayer. What is adequate? When we pray, we enter the realm of God. When we talk about God, we step into the language of poetry, of fiction. The action of God may be translated as like an eagle, a tailor, a potter, a shepherd, and a fortress. Metaphors are not neutral. God as a male King is a familiar symbol of status and power. It indicates ownership and obedience and social distance. This figurative language is the product—understandably—of a social history. But most religions also use concepts of God as an Absolute, Oneness and Spirit. Julian of Norwich in the fourteenth century simultaneously

---

3. Unterman, *Wisdom of the Jewish Mystics*, 58–59.
4. Buber, quoted in Shonkoff, "Metanomianism and Religious Praxis."

referred God as he and she and invokes ideas of motherhood as well as fatherhood. There are alternatives that intensify the personal above sex. The idea of the "kindness" of God prioritizes friendship and the familial, suggests Janet Martin Soskice in the appropriately titled *The Kindness of God* (2007), and refers to the Middle English usage of "kinde," which includes kinship.

Our words of address—"Almighty God!," "Eternal Father!," etc.—are one thing. Our spoken and silent words of prayer are another. Gender-specific language should not trouble the person who prays. We must think linguistically; to be aware that languages and their unique grammars lock us into their limited systems. A pronoun-heavy language like English is a forced-choice language. The grammar and vocabulary may compel us to choose "he," "she" or "it" even when we prefer otherwise, as in, "Listen, Aisling, I'm telling you. God is genderless. He really is." It helps if you use a gender-neutral language (unmarked) for third-person pronouns. Many languages do this, like the various deaf sign languages or Asian and Finno-Ugric languages.

Bad Sorrow

Prayer almost always addresses sorrow. We own our sorrow. It is good to make space and embrace it. Sorrow can make us better, stronger. Much of our sorrow seems to be of no help to us. It doesn't create a better future. It doesn't help put things right. Bad sorrow dwells incessantly upon a bad past that cannot be put right. Bad sorrow shakes its head over an act of misjudgment, a deplorable error that still damages me.

We pray because we are at some stage of sorrow. The sixteenth-century divine Richard Hooker, in his sermon "A Learned and Comfortable Sermon of the Certainty and Perpetuity of Faith in the Elect" (1585), drew attention to those persons in the "extremity of grief" who "find not themselves in themselves: they cannot find what is actually within them, and lament as for a thing which is past finding . . ."[5] Prayer gives us the courage to see ourselves not as deplorable persons and prayer is not an opportunity for bad sorrow. Our mistakes reveal an incapacity, an imperfection. In pray we gather up the past simply as things done well or not well. The future is an opportunity toward renewal. From the grammar of past negative passive—"things not done"—to future positive active—"things I will do."

The Communion of Mortals

The supreme form of life energy is the other person. This life energy derives from what Nikolai Nikolaevich, the beloved uncle of Yuri Zhivago in Boris Pasternak's *Dr. Zhivago*, called the "immortal communion among mortals."[6] The moment we commit to the prayer we place ourselves in the immortals of the past and present. In the same work—a novel of trains and railway lines and junctions—a solitary Lara, waiting at the train station, understands for the first time that to travel is to make connections between people: people that we are always leaving and meeting. We are destined to make sense of things and people and that they all have their own names, just like stations. We all possess a fierce magic that unites us as persons. And from what does this magic derive? A love of life.

Prayer is a human endeavor when we are alone, when we are in a crowd. We pray with other persons even when they are not there. Prayer in a physical group can be risky when it morphs into a string of loud collective demands to the Almighty—this and that and the other. Every prayer must be focused on my reconciliation with God, with myself—God's work of art—and with the world of others.

Many persons find power and meaning within the communion of the church—in its beauty and noble traditions, in its holy people, in the turning of the liturgical year, its theologies that strive ever upward to capture our divine experience. Other persons are

---

5. Williams, *Anglican Identities*, 62.
6. Pasternak, *Doctor Zhivago*.

metanomian. They live reverently on the edge of established religion, identifying the essence of religious understanding (or non-understanding) as "outside any fixed system without necessarily opposing the system as a matter of principle."[7] This includes religious thinkers of great philosophical and theological power, like Martin Buber or Simone Weil, who did not adhere, respectively, to Jewish law or Christian practice as a binding code.

Being in the Right Place

What do we want from prayer? If prayer battles for space in our lives is it worth the struggle? Compare the Greek (Socratic) goal of cool self-knowledge with the Jewish (Abrahamic) vision of promise whereby we wait. We await a transformation, a re-creation, a resurrection.

In prayer we want simply, to use a well-known phrase, for our hearts to be in the right place. That is all. What the heart loves is what the mind will follow. The rest will follow. What can I do about the dilemmas I face every day? Well we think it's a kind of war. Keep calm and carry on. My troubled life. But life is not war. Prayer can give us new heart: to carry on. To encourage each other and our collective well-being. To cultivate a new path. Prayer travels in two directions. God and me. God with me. Prayer is often silent, unspoken. Prayer trains me in this interdependence. It is a reflection of my interdependence with others. This intertwining makes me who I am.

Prayer renews relations. Our relationship with God is the model of all our relations with others. It is not utilitarian. It is a life-giving relation among persons, in Martin Buber's classic formulation, an I-Thou rather than I-It.[8] This relation is not a means to an end. Our meeting with God—in nature and aesthetic experience, through revelation, through others—is a unifying event. We know it is because it sends us new life, airborne and glistening.

7. Shonkoff, "Metanomianism and Religious Praxis," 1.
8. See Buber, *I and Thou*.

4

Prayers

Prayer to an All-Gendered God: Beyond Words

ALMIGHTY GOD. YOU ARE the Divine Mystery of life. You speak to us on sunny days, on cold winter walks, taking a shower, standing on a train. When I sense the presence of God I do not sense a man or a woman or in-between. You are not beyond gender or genderless. You are a unifier. You are all and every gender. That is how I want to talk to You.

Almighty God You are a unifier. You help us see the material differences of our world as flowing together. These differences are part of a single language, a new articulation. You are the mystery of integration in the midst of separation. Going deeper into the mystery of God I arrive at a still place described in many religions of the world—sometimes Father or Lord or King or Mother or Goddess. Sometimes Running Stream, Liberator, Shepherd, Night Watchman. You are a holy place where things come together: the unifier. So, just for today I will call it the Sacred Heart.

> As one whom his mother comforts,
> so I will comfort you. (Isa 66:13, NIV)

You revealed Your identity a long time ago.

> I am who I am. (Exod 3:14)

That's OK with me. It's expansive. I want to connect with Your be-ing.

Almighty God You are full of gender. You are inside everything. You are the spirit of animals and birds and insects, of him and her and them and me. God is our Father or our Mother and other names. It's a tradition. I've got it. It makes sense. It comes from somewhere and sometime. The essence is my mysterious relation at the very center of my life in the Sacred Heart.

God of strength and peace You restore my soul.

Prayer against Pessimism: Dark Mind, Bright Heart

Almighty God. Optimism is part of nature. It sees a glass half full. Optimism is trust and I trust but dark comes easy. I'm pessimistic. Then I'm optimistic. You don't seem to mind. Are You teasing me? Perhaps they are both the fruits of one tree, one branch. Keeping going. Being optimistic is good.

> Be strong and courageous. Do not be frightened, and do not be dismayed, for the Lord your God is with you wherever you go. (Josh 1:9)

I am comforted by this. I'm optimistic when I keep moving, looking up, looking forward. There is continuity. I have what I need.

> With joy you will draw water from the wells of salvation. (Isa 12:3)

You urge me to think the best and keep on my feet. This is not a lost road. It might be the right place to be.

Pessimists are often right but don't they die young? Optimism is not cockeyed. Optimists take care of their health. They build an extra muscle of positive thinking. Almighty God, help me reframe my situation. Every calamity will be overcome. Help me react better to failure. Always think about the next thing.

> Surely goodness and mercy shall follow me all the days of my life, and I shall dwell in the house of the LORD forever. (Ps 23:6)

God of strength and peace You restore my soul.

Prayer of a Liar: Take Me Up

Almighty God. I am a liar. False talk. "Misrepresentation" is my game. I don't do any harm. And, hey, I'm not the only one. People lie all the time. I just put a spin on things. I lie for harmony's sake. After all, liars were heroes in ancient Greece. Better a lie that than the brutal truth? No. I've got it wrong again.

When I tell too many lies I can no longer recognize the truth. I'm not living for real. Most of the time I believe it's in the interest of others. I know what You're thinking, "Yeah, sure."

> These are the things that you shall do: Speak the truth to one another; render in your gates judgments that are true and make for peace. (Zech 8:16)

I know there is one sure method for avoiding lies and lying. Keep my mouth shut. Listen more. What are people really saying? What do they want? What are their hopes and fears?

The highest good is the good of the person. This may involve lies but I promise not to get in deep. A lie takes me down. Please take me up. The truth sets me free, forever.

> Truthful lips endure forever, but a lying tongue is but for a moment. (Prov 12:19)

I'll try to taste the sweetness of the truth. I will start by being true to myself. Just for today.

God of strength and peace You restore my soul.

Prayer for Hope: A Unique Wisdom

Almighty God. You breathed life into human beings and sent them into a mysterious world. It is a world full of sound and fury. It makes me tremble every day. What's going to go wrong today?

> Be strong and courageous. Do not fear or be in dread of them, for it is the Lord your God who goes with you. He will not leave you or forsake you. (Deut 31:6, *NIV*)

You placed in this world a unique wisdom. You inserted hope within each human heart . It helps us make sense of everything. It is a fortress inside that never ages and nothing can destroy. You gave this place a name, "the Kingdom of God." In the Kingdom of God, hope is my source of wisdom. Especially when I am incomprehensible to myself.

> I will say to the LORD, "My refuge and my fortress, My God, in whom I trust!" (Ps 91:2)

Pessimism is a spiritual virus killed by hope. Hope is the final frontier. In this moment I cannot hope that this and that will happen for the better. I just hope. I can't know tomorrow or the next day. Merely to hope is enough. In my despair I deny the world. In my hope I look at its face in a clear light. My hope is my guide, my castle on the hill, my kindly light, the beating holy spirit within. My hope is divine grace.

God of strength and peace You restore my soul.

Prayer for My Religion: Goodness and Misery

My faith sometimes feels like a small room in a big world. It does its best through the daily efforts of good people and of historic institutions. My religion is humane and heroic. It works day and night in the streets, in hospitals and prisons and schools. It works for the poor and the rich and oppressed. It is a place and a space in my life.

My religion is sometimes uncomfortable. My church lacks the good qualities that some other churches, some other religions, possess. I seek forgiveness for the terrible mistakes of religions, yesterday and today, when religions harass, murder and destroy in Your holy name. This is the work of human hands. Those hands have touched pitch. I acknowledge it.

My faith is what I have. Its traditions go back thousands of years and through many generations of the faithful.

My faith is an eternal flame. It lights my way. It warms me.

> And the angel of the LORD appeared to him in a flame of fire out of the midst of a bush. He looked, and behold, the bush was burning, yet it was not consumed. (Exod 3:2)

Almighty God. Instill the leaders of my faith with two passions. A passion for life here and now and a passion for eternal life. Renew the rules of religions to promote mercy and justice among its members. Guide the faithful of my religion along the right path.

My faith gives me confidence not fear. In my faith I do not fear the sound of Your footsteps. I do not fear death or hell. I look forward with lightness of heart. My faith teaches me that the graveyard is the house of life.

God of strength and peace You restore my soul.

Prayer of a Mother and Father: The Grace of Children

I give thanks. My children are my renewal. In them a perfect unity has been achieved. In them history has become real. Their coming throws a bridge across time. Now I count time by generations. Grandparents, parents, us, and now you! Oh, my child!

I will make traditions to shelter you, make a home, make you at home. I will be an example. I will train and equip and encourage you, hold you tight and let you go.

> All your children shall be taught by the Lord,
> and great shall be the peace of your children.
> (Isa 54:13, NIV)

Almighty God. I hope my child will make good choices and look to You sometimes.

> For you, O Lord, are my hope, my trust, O Lord, from my youth. (Ps 71:5)

I am anxious. This child overwhelms me. I have already made bad decisions. Can I get it right tomorrow? I know that I must move my thoughts to generosity and good humor. Help me to forgive my child and to forgive myself for my many mistakes and foolish words.

God of strength and peace You restore my soul.

Prayer of a Person Who Cannot Pray: Keeping in Touch with Eternity

Prayer is beyond time. By praying I step into eternity. I need it. When I'm praying it seems a waste of time. It's a sluggish stream of words. It's lifeless repetition. A bundle of dry sticks. I can hear them snap.

Almighty God. I know that my discontent is just fine with You. Because in this desert of dryness You are there waiting, watching, listening. So, I will do what I can. It's not even my best. You do not ask me to feel good, or feel bad, think this way, or that way.

You just want me to want You.

> You God are my God,
> earnestly I seek you;
> I thirst for you,
> my whole being longs for you,
> in a dry and parched land
> where there is no water. (Ps 63:1)

Almighty God. You want my will. You want me with or without a conversation. You've got it. Union with You. Solidarity. I promise to try to speak to You sometimes—with a simple prayer. I promise not to speak to You sometimes—and just be still.

When I cannot pray and cannot touch You I know that I am in touch with You. I'll keep going.

> Because you are my help, I sing in the shadow of your wings. (Ps 63:7)

God of strength and peace You restore my soul.

Prayer of the Unemployed: The Work of My Hands

Almighty God. You know I just don't know. I'm worn out looking for work. The rejections. Why? Check the boxes. I'm in the wrong place, the wrong time, sickness, my face, disability, discrimination, bad luck, laziness, crappy references, don't ask good questions, can't explain my past, no network, dress badly, I'm negative, underqualified, overqualified, didn't do my research, don't seem enthusiastic, the competition!

I'm unemployed. I have people to support. I am a decent person. I have strengths and abilities. I have skills.

> Let the favor of the Lord our God be upon us,
> and establish the work of our hands upon us. (Ps 90:17)

Let me see myself beyond the rejections. I want a society where people can experience the joy of work, for the good of the world, to work and enjoy life.

> All hard work brings a profit, but mere talk leads only to poverty. (Prov 14:23)

Look with pity on those who cannot work, who have no job. Let me look beyond the rejections. Almighty God, calm my fear—no, it's panic. I am not a failure because I have no job. I want to contribute to society, to the common good. I want to grow as a person.

> So I saw that there is nothing better than that a man should rejoice in his work, for that is his lot. Who can bring him to see what will be after him? (Eccl 3:22, NLT)

God of strength and peace You restore my soul.

Prayers

Prayer of an Administrator: Following the Mission

Almighty God. I am proud of my work. I'm an administrator. I have ideals. I want a decent society for all people. I know I have a grave duty. I know there are competive visions of society. In the rough-and-tumble of my work I want to build a consensus that everyone can own. And whatever vision we choose, the governance of this world must be in accord with divine mercy and justice.

I know that I should not have power over but power under. I am a servant. I serve and make changes for the better. Perhaps I can be an agent of grace. That power originates with You. The only power that makes a difference is You.

> God changes times and seasons; he removes kings and sets up kings; he gives wisdom to the wise and knowledge to those who have understanding. (Dan 2:21)

Help me keep my determination to care—for people, about people. Light the flame of desire in my heart. Help me renew my mission for all citizens and listen to their voices.

I'm human. Sometimes I don't care. What the hell. I am a master of excuses. Give me the wisdom to step outside my own world into the shoes of a waiter and a taxi driver, a nurse and a teacher, a homeless person and a farmer.

> Like a roaring lion and a rushing bear is a wicked ruler over a poor people. (Prov 28:15)

Almighty God. I have influence. I am a force for good. I will make the best effort with humility and prayer. I am the hand of God. When thinking about people's livelihood how can I make a God-shaped difference?

I am an ordinary person who can accomplish God's work. To make perfect the world that God has created. I will be modest. The fate of this society does not all depend of me. This is a comfort. Stay with me.

God of strength and peace You restore my soul.

Prayer before Mess: Kondo-ing My Spiritual Life

Almighty God. I need to Kondo my life. It's a mess. No, I'm a mess. I am dependent on so many material things. I amass them. Owning them is not really the problem. It's my attachment to them. They keep me company.

I depend on negative thoughts. I amass them. They overtake my life. Shame and guilt for instance. Memories of dumb things I have done. They last a lifetime. I keep them there. I can't move on. Still there? Do I really need you anymore? Yes, I should find something good to put in its place.

I know that simplicity is a holy path towards You. There is "stuff" blocking my way. Some of my clutter has sentimental value but it still weighs heavily on me. The mess is there because of my indecision. "I will put them away!" I procrastinate. "Later."

Messiness is the life I have made for myself. Time to declutter. Time to clean up. I look at the things around me. They start as things, then become friends. In time some of them start to carry a special spirit. God's little things.

> The LORD preserveth the simple:
> When I was brought low, and he saved me. (Ps 116:6)

I look at the mountain of unloved things in my life—grudges stacked up, brooding thoughts like the mess on my floor. But even the unloved and unlovely things in my life have a purpose. I bow my head. I will acknowledge them and send them on their way.

God of strength and peace You restore my soul.

Prayer of the Traveler: Each Journey Is a Pilgrimage

Almighty God. I travel today through Your world. It is a world of beauty and misery. Through lands of enchantment, over fields and seas, over cities of war and peace. I will step outside of my own world. Travel is a pilgrimage. You are everywhere. You never leave us.

> He leads me in paths of righteousness
> for his name's sake.
> Even though I walk through the valley of the shadow of death,
> I will fear no evil. (Ps 23:3–4)

Give me the joy of travel, the delight in new places, the smells and sights of roads and mountains. Keep me safe. Guardian angel, be my guide, stay by my side, watch my steps.

> For he will command his angels concerning you
> to guard you in all your ways. (Ps 91:11–12)

Almighty God. I set out from my home and I will return. As I move from place to place I am exhilarated, anxious, sometimes terrified. I am only human. Watch over me. Calm me. Calm my anxiety. Watch my back. Hold my hand. Smooth my path.

Each journey is a learning. Along the path I will see the strangeness, the misery and wonders of this world. Stay with me.

God of strength and peace You restore my soul.

Prayer before Meals

Bread of the earth, fruit of the tree
through God's creation all things came to be
For this food we give You thanks.

5

On Praying

The Divine Milieu: Love Actually

EACH PERSON IS "TUNED" to holiness. We are not sure what scale it is: presumably *musica divina*. We know that we are naturally tuned to the divine because we know core things of the interior life—love and compassion. They are the real thing. Priest and paleontologist Teilhard de Chardin termed this core *le milieu divin*. It is powerful and overwhelming. Life comes from the physical world, which our minds and bodies are part of. The physical act of prayer—kneeling, joining hands, crossing the threshold of a holy place—expresses the unity of nature. Chardin holds that it is our interior life—our spiritual experience, *vie intérieure*—that makes physical experience meaningful—not the other way round.[1]

We don't need a manual to inform us that we are in the presence of love: when a newborn child wraps its fingers around ours, when we contemplate a twilight sky in summer, when we stand remembering in a graveyard. We are "designed" for the spirit and are kept there only by love. It is the core of Being.

Prayer is being together with living things. Another word for such being together is "compassion." This means compassion for

---

1. Chardin, *Le Milieu divin*, 74.

the everyday—for the workplace, the desk, cooking and cleaning, riding the train to work, studying, getting up in the morning and lying down at night. When we conform to these acts, when we submit ourselves to them, we have compassion.

Pots-'n-pans compassion works in the daily life of convents and monasteries and religious houses throughout the world. It is reverential. In those places it is known as (an expression strange to outsiders) "a life of prayer."

Compassion for things is the core of the religious life—especially in monasteries and convents—focusing on the daily round of life. Prayer can be defined as being together with all beings, with the world. What this means is that by becoming one with the pot-'n-pans ourselves we become whole.

Doing the simple acts of everyday life, deliberately, this is the beginning and ending of prayer. These rituals of life are made special and beautiful in different religious traditions throughout the world. Daily rituals help me lead an ethical life. It is our decision to be attentive or not. That is the message of the great Christian prayer of Jesus. Things are put there/here "to be done." This is what we do.

The Rose Window of York: Many Parts Make a Whole

My wandering prayers go here and there among a crowd of people and things and events. They are all gathered up in one exquisite center. Just like the concealed center of a rose.

In Europe, the builders of medieval cathedrals, like France's Reims Cathedral or Italy's Siena, inserted in one particular wall is a stained-glass "rose window." This circular *oculus* or "eye" window is made from spokes radiating from a central opening. It's a hole. Curiously, at first sight, it resembles a multipetalled rose. Surrounding the window—often in Islamic-style stonework—there are scenes from everyday life or narratives from the Bible, or bestiaries.

There is a rose window at York Minster in the north of England. It is cohesive and subdivided into scores of smaller windows. We strain our eyes at the sacred geometry. The still point at the center. The point of perfect balance. Each tiny window petal derives beauty from the next one. Light from the Yorkshire sky pours in. On the ground at the foot of the window there is wooden box. I read a notice that says, "Every day in the Minster there are services and times of prayer. If there is something or someone you would like us to pray for, then we invite you write your request . . ." Commitment to the other person is meant to be as bars of stone in the rose window that connect us to other persons. Others. The blue card concludes with a prayer: "Heavenly Father, we commit ourselves and those we love to your care this day, praying that you will guard us from danger and guide us in the right way."

Daydreams are real. The presence of others involves the dead, the living, family, friends and strangers. They are all gathered up. We look at stuff left undone, the zigzags and unspoken sorrows of the day. These are gathered up. We gather up childhood. Fragments of prayers sit still in our memory until suddenly one day an old hymn from school assembly sits up in your mind and you whistle it walking on the road. By praying and keeping faith with prayer we go to the making of a good past.

Sacred Waters

Washing is a kind of subtraction. We remove superfluous things: from our body, from the day, from work, from life. We bring the stain of the day with us, to prayer. Why hide it? And then we show respect and resolve by putting our hands in water. The earth's sweet being will wash it away.

Washing before prayer is practiced in most of the world's religions. In many Christian churches there is a water stoop—a *bénitier*—at the entrance. Muslims wash before prayer—the ritual washing of *wudhu*. In Japan, the *chozuya* is a big stone basin at the entrance of temples and shrines. With long wooden dippers you purify your hands with cool flowing water before entering sacred ground. Water is holy because of what we do, what we make it do.

Fountains for washing hands and feet were made ready for pilgrims at the Greek Orthodox monasteries of Mt. Athos. The use of holy water is a practice that Martin Luther called an opportunity for a "reaffirmation" of faith. Washing is both a removal and a return to an earlier state; emptying the jug, restoring the hands to cleanliness. Holy water, Luther urged, is an outward sign of an inner affirmation. "I wash my hands in innocence and go around your altar, O Lord," (Ps 26:6). It is a little rebaptism.

Washing before prayer has a sacramental meaning. Washing is an outward sign of an inner change. Washing is taking something away—ready for action—and therefore a kind of emptying. The spirit moves over the waters and rests upon me.

Where Feelings Begin

Beat poet and Anglican monastic Kenneth Rexroth argued that the foundation of prayer is *kenōsis*: "this is where the religious experience begins. The vessel must be emptied before it can be filled."[2] *Kenōsis*—an emptying—is a familiar term in religious thought. It is a motif in Greek philosophy—in Plato's *Republic*—and, of course, in Greek medicine: Hippocrates' invention of "purgation"—the removal of excess. To pray is to be honest. It is to start from nothing. I recognize that I came into life with nothing and I will go to death with nothing. With hope and with no hope. With expectation and with no expectation. When we pray, then, we are completely open, *kenotic*. This emptiness is a kind of death and death is kenosis' supreme expression.

In prayer I give my time and place, with no hope of immediate solution and consolation, but something stronger with the suppleness of the power of steel. It is power of hope itself.

Three Women's Prayers:
Courage, Gratitude and Tranquility

Prayers speak to different ends—as the prayers in this collection indicate. We can learn much about how to pray by listening to the prayers of others. The different purposes of prayer can be illustrated

---

2. Rexroth, *With Eye and Ear*, 123.

by three women at different times and places: Deborah (twelfth century BC), Mary (first century AD), Teresa (sixteenth century).

"Deborah's Song" was written in the twelfth century BC: a blistering prayer of courage in the face of impossible odds. Beware. The story is not pretty. It's war. Deborah was priestess and prophet in premonarchic Israel. The only woman judge in the Bible, Deborah was renowned for her fairness and openness. The most famous woman of the Hebrew Bible, described in the book of Judges 4–5, Deborah was also renowned as a wise leader and military commander. She led Israel in battle to free the people from oppression and slavery by the Canaanites, facing off her opponent, General Sisera, and his "nine hundred chariots of iron." Deborah's prayer begins as morning breaks on the day of conflict. She prays an exhortation to her justifiably terrified commander, Barak. The message behind this mission impossible is "to trust in God who knows," "who is"—the past, the present and future—and who has "gone ahead of you." She finishes with a bold battle cry, in Joan of Arc fashion. "So may all your enemies perish, O Lord! But your friends be like the sun as he rises in his might" (Judg 5:31). Read the story. We conclude that the real enemy, as Deborah concludes, is our own fear, the fear of freedom, our fear *de jour*.

A different type of prayer is "Mary's Song," a prayer of gratitude, known in the Latin world as the "Magnificat" and in the Orthodox Church as the "Ode of the Theotokos." From the first century AD, the Magnificat is recorded in the Gospel of Luke (1:46–55). It was a declaration by Mary, the mother of Jesus, on the occasion of her visit to Elizabeth, her cousin. Mary, young and virgin, is pregnant with Jesus. Elizabeth, old and childless, is pregnant with John the Baptist. Something was going on there. Out of the ordinary. Mary's song is full of words of delight and thanks. "My soul doth magnify the Lord. And my spirit hath rejoiced in God my Savior" (Luke 1:46–55, KJV).

Prayers of peace and tranquility are a universal genre. The sixteenth-century Carmelite nun Teresa of Avila was a religious reformer and theologian who also wrote prayers and poems. She composed in tumultuous times of plague, persecution and war but

On Praying

her prayers were marked by an unfailing tranquility.[3] For a prayer for times of distress, about the permanence of God, this is a classic of the period. It starts thus:

> Let nothing perturb you. Let nothing make you fearful.
> All things pass, Only God does not change.
> Patience gains everything.
> Have God and you will want nothing more.

The Vatican administrator the time, exasperated by Teresa, dubbed her *femina inquieta, andariega, desobediente y contumaz*, "a noisy woman, gregarious, disobedient and contumacious."[4]

The prayers of Deborah, Mary and Teresa sail like birds across time and worlds. They are poems of mission impossible, illustrating the classic themes of prayer: courage, gratitude and tranquility.

---

3. For the original Spanish read Wikisource's "Nada te turbe."
4. Adalid, "Santa Teresa y la Inquisición."

6

Prayers

Prayer of a Dying Person: Gratitude

Almighty God. Why me? Why now? I don't understand why things happen the way they do. I don't have answers.

This body. My body! Oh, temple of the spirit! Friend. You served me well. May I never lose my gratitude for life.

> Praise the LORD, my soul, and forget not all his benefits—who forgives all your sins and heals all your diseases, who redeems your life from the pit and crowns you with love and compassion. (Ps 103:2–4)

Calm my panic. Ease my fear. Give me courage. This illness does not kill hope or memories. It will not destroy friendship. It cannot harm other people. It happens to everyone. They know that.

My earthly pilgrimage is coming to an end. I'm in the departure lounge, continuing my journey, the next leg, to heaven and eternal life. I want to see what comes next.

> The Lord protects and preserves them—
> they are counted among the blessed in the land—
> The Lord sustains them on their sickbed
> and restores them from their bed of illness. (Ps 41:2–3)

My family, friend, nurses and doctors care for me. Make me a bridge for other dying people in this place to cross over. Even now, I can help heal others.

The last word at the end of life? Gratitude.

God of strength and peace You restore my soul.

Prayer of a Student: The Beat Goes On

Almighty God I look for purpose in my study because I look for purpose in my life. College is awesome. I'm learning. New knowledge. New skills. People challenge me. They question my thinking. I am grateful to them.

University is amazing. It holds within its walls the wisdom of humankind. It's a privilege many people in my country will never have. I am grateful. I owe the people who built and sustained this college. I owe the people who helped put me here. I will honor their effort.

> Hold on to instruction, do not let it go; guard it well, for it is your life. (Prov 4:13)

My school has a heartbeat. When I meet good teachers and good classmates I hear it. When I read a book that opens a window onto the world I hear it. When I sit in a class that takes me on a journey of discovery I hear it. The heartbeat. Across time, through the history of this great place. The beat goes on. Now it's my turn.

I'm worried about a lot of things. Grades, falling behind, relationships, avoiding distractions, dumb stuff and dangerous stuff. OK. The checklist. Study diligently. Seek advice when you need it. Organize the day, the semester. Eat and sleep responsibly. Take time to relax and seek serenity. Is that too much? Can I get through it? Yeah.

> Do not forsake wisdom, and she will protect you; love her, and she will watch over you. The beginning of wisdom is this: Get wisdom. Though it cost all you have, get understanding. (Prov 4:6–7)

I will take each collision, each fall, with good grace. Failure will help me. I'm work in progress. I'll get motivated.

I want to do more than survive. I want to grow and flourish and prosper. I can become a responsible citizen. I can become a better person.

God of strength and peace You restore my soul.

Prayer of a Homeless Person: Give Us a Future

Almighty God. I have no permanent residence. I live where I can, how I can.

I want people to know that I am a real person, in a difficult situation. I know that some homeless choose this way.

We spend our nights in doorways, in parks and sometimes shelters. We wander in the streets. I am always afraid. Perplexed. We need shelter, food and water. We want a smile and a kind word. It makes a difference. Above all we want hope.

There are homeless people everywhere in the world. We are what we are for many reasons. We come from broken families, unemployment, drug addiction, sickness, relatives who no longer care.

Almighty God. I have a name. I have a past. Give us Your protection. Give us a future.

Your love extends to all people: of ethnicity, gender, social background. Although it seems we are outside society we are inside Your love. Heal our broken hearts. Lift us up. Send me forward.

God of strength and peace You restore my soul.

Prayer of an Addict: Roads to Freedom

Almighty God. I want freedom. I am trapped inside the madness of this thing. It demolishes my time and money and concentration. It has hijacked my brain.

I brought agony to my life. The people in my life deserve an apology. I'm going make it. Not easy.

I'm diseased by addiction. What is life for? This? I am a prisoner. Take me out of this prison. Lead me away. Cleanse my senses. They are sick. My poor body. Friend! Wait! Forgive me! Take me on the road that leads out and away. I will seek help. Now. Not easy. But I will set my feet on a journey to recovery.

Almighty God, inspire my thinking and decisions. I want to be a victor not a victim. I have plans. I will find good friends not bad ones. I will seek pleasure and happiness elsewhere. Yes. I will look for help. I will.

Almighty God. You have a plan. Your plan is entitled "life."

> For I know the plans I have for you, declares the Lord, plans for welfare[a] and not for evil, to give you a future and a hope. (Jer 29:11)

God of strength and peace You restore my soul.

Prayer of a Single Parent: My Child Inspires Me

Almighty God. All my life is known to You. I am a single parent. You know the whys and hows. Single people carry their own cross. They walk up a steep hill. I cannot be everywhere, do everything. I am often overwhelmed. Asking for help hurts me. I need compassion not pity. I don't want any more sorry faces, especially mine. And just now what I want is not a spouse but more hours in the day.

My child inspires me. Friends support me. I can live. There are good people in my child's life who can teach them and guide them and be good examples. I can work and pay the bills. I am grateful.

Almighty God, I am grateful. I can call upon You because You called me.

> When you pass through the waters, I will be with you,
> and through the rivers, they will not overflow you.
> When you walk through the fire, you will not be scorched,
> nor will the flame burn you. (Isa 43:1–2)

Keep me strong and healthy. Give me confidence in my child and in myself.

God of strength and peace You restore my soul.

Prayer of the Body: Feelin' Good

Almighty God. My precious body is my friend. It accompanies me, faithfully, day by day. The spirit of God breathes through me with every breath I take. My body wants peace and respect. It's beautiful. Sensuality, pride in my appearance, my sexuality. These are Your gifts.

When I feel good it's very good. When I feel bad I treat my body with contempt. My body frustrates me. It controls me. It should be the other way round. I hate my weakness, the aches and pains and illness.

Health and sickness, old age and death. The pilgrimage You arranged for me. You comfort me.

> I am the Lord, your healer. (Exod 15: 26)

Almighty God. My body tells me what's going on in my mind. My body has wisdom that I lack. It is a window of my soul.

> For I am fearfully and wonderfully made.
> Wonderful are your works;
> my soul knows it very well.
> My frame was not hidden from you,
> when I was being made in secret,
> intricately woven in the depths of the earth.
> (Ps 139:13–16)

Almighty God. You created my body as precious not repulsive. My precious body! My friend!

God of strength and peace You restore my soul.

Prayer of Joy: A Life Worth Loving

Almighty God. The world is worth loving. You know it doesn't come easy in the violent and unjust place I am. But I sing the children's song, "Count your blessings. Name them one by one. Count your blessings. See what God has done!"

Life is worth living. I burden myself with regret. "Could have. Should have." But I will throw such weight overboard, sailing forward not looking back. Life is lighter when it's joyful.

The meaning of life is giving thanks. Even when I don't mean it. Grateful is what I want to be. To learn from the strength and thirst for life I see in people around me. They teach me that the world is worth loving.

> Lord, you alone are my inheritance, my cup of blessing.
> You guard all that is mine. The land you have given me is
> a pleasant land. What a wonderful inheritance!
> (Ps 16:5–6, NLT)

Almighty God. I am grateful for life. Maybe I'm supposed to get more out of life than it takes out of me. I want to make a happier space for myself and for other people. I want to give back to society what I have received. With thanks. Life is better when it's joyful. And joy is an act of courage.

God of strength and peace You restore my soul.

Prayer to the Holy Spirit: Switching Me On

The Holy Spirit is the memory of God in us. I have it. It's a lot of gigabytes. Plug it in. This memory starts up my longing for God.

> And the Spirit of God was hovering over the face of the
> waters. (Gen 1:2)

The Holy Spirit is my only proof that I come from the supernatural world. Start me up.

> The Spirit of God has made me,
> and the breath of the Almighty gives me life.
> (Job 33:4)

The Holy Spirit switches me on, uniting the spiritual and the material. When lifeless matter receives the breath it becomes real. I am real in the lifespan of my own body. But it doesn't last forever. How could it? I wouldn't want it to.

Then the LORD said, "My Spirit will not contend with humans forever, for they are mortal. (Gen 6:3)

The Holy Spirit is the proof of God in me. The Holy Spirit is power. The power that give wings to the dove. The power that makes me live in my body. It floats above it like a dove hovering over a river. Transcendence.

The Holy Spirit is knowledge of God's presence. The pure desire for God. A living thing breathes. It thinks and moves. A dead thing is still and silent. Plug me into the memory of God in me.

I will pour out my Spirit on every person. (Joel 2:28)

God of strength and peace You restore my soul.

Prayer of an Envious Person: Turning to Thankfulness

Almighty God. I am an envious person. It damages my peace of mind. I am envious of his position, her achievements. I look at them and my soul squints. Funny, I'm not envious of celebrities; only about people like me and near me. I'm happy at their misfortune, dismayed at their success. I can do that better than them. Yes. It's pride. The other side of envy.

Almighty God. I am sorry for all this. I know there is a way out of my rotten envy. It's gratitude. Thankfulness for what I have. Thankfulness will give me peace.

A tranquil heart gives life to the flesh,
but envy makes the bones rot. (Prov 14:30, NIV)

Almighty God. Envy puts me deep in the mire. Face down. Those I envy fill me up, become part of me. It's menacing but it's what I want. No. It's not what I want. I'm not me anymore. I let them take me over. I turned myself into a victim, a different person. It's not the person I should be. I created an idol. I want myself back.

> You must not make for yourself an idol of any kind or an image of anything in the heavens or on the earth or in the sea. You must not bow down to them or worship them (Exod 20:4–6, NLT)

I know that we are imitators by nature. But I am discontented. I realize that this feeling is a kind of sorrow. This feeling will not end well. King David had everything he wanted in the world. And he wanted more. So he committed murder by proxy to get it. I do that too. I am envious so I murder them by criticism, rumor, slander and smears.

> You shall not covet your neighbor's house. (Exod 20:17)

Almighty God. Thankfulness. Other people's accomplishments do not damage my life. Thankfulness. I will make a commitment. When they succeed I will rejoice—or just stay calm.

> This is the day which the Lord has made; Let us rejoice and be glad in it. (Ps 118:24)

Help me to be thankful. I have more than I deserve. Help me calm down, do what I can do, become tranquil. I give thanks.
God of strength and peace You restore my soul.

Prayer of a Person Harassed: Freedom from Domination

I am harassed. It makes me sick. Thinking about it makes me depressed. Humiliated. I know my reaction is normal. Anger.

> He heals the broken-hearted and binds up their wounds. (Ps 147:3)

It happened to me. It was wrong. It was illegal. It's created a hostile environment. I feel broken. Can I do something about this? Yes, I can. My story is a common one. We take back control.

I will free myself from this domination. I will not stay stuck. I will take back control. I will rest this bad memory while I take action. I'll talk to a safe person. I'll stay connected. I'll keep a diary. I will set down how this is affecting me. I'll find a support group.

I know there are honorable people. (Don't we want everyone to be honorable?) I will communicate with people I trust. I won't close up. I won't turn inside and turn on myself. That's it. Communicate!

Almighty God. I have seen the darkness. No. I am inside it. Separate me from that darkness. Help me stay connected. Set my feet on the road out. Put me in the light. That is Your purpose for me. That is what You made life for.

> God saw that the light was good. And God separated the light from the darkness. (Gen 1:4)

God of strength and peace You restore my soul.

Prayer of Dismay about Government: Best Practice in the Family of Nations

Almighty God. I am dismayed. This politics is not so good or maybe it's just despicable. How come? How did it get this way? How did I get this way? Was I, am I responsible?

I am not alone. There are decent people who share my unhappiness. There are administrators, men and women, who share my disappointment. There are politicians, men and women, who are dignified and honorable. We are grateful for them.

Government is there. People put it there. But only the goodness and kindness of a government will sustain it.

> Steadfast love and faithfulness preserve the king,
> and by steadfast love his throne is upheld. (Prov 20:27)

There are people who share my desire for change.

> It is an abomination to kings to do evil,
> for the throne is established by righteousness.
> (Prov 16:12)

This nation is not alone. We are members of the family of nations. There are universal laws of justice and integrity. Let us look to other countries and their systems for best practice. Let's search our traditions and successes for wisdom.

Almighty God. Give us leaders with hearts that weep for justice. Give us leaders that feel the horror of the poverty of citizens. Give us leaders that protect our work and health and environment. Give us leaders that we respect because of their kindness and intelligence.

> For wisdom will come into your heart, and knowledge
> will be pleasant to your soul. (Prov 2:10)

Give us leaders with compassion and integrity.
God of strength and peace You restore my soul.

Prayer of a Person Who Lost Faith: Walking Away, Walking Back

Almighty God. My faith was damaged. You know what happens. Maybe no reasons. I don't know. There are reasons. Setbacks, abuse, deep hurt. It crushes your dreams. There's righteous anger. You walk away. You cover your ears.

> I will restore to you the years that the swarming locust
> has eaten. (Joel 2:25)

I've lost my faith. Maybe I needed that to happen. Your faith dives under. It looks on you with mercy. It puts its hand on your shoulder. It stands waiting like an angel. No, pushing and pulling. I know it takes time for faith to make itself known again.

Almighty God. Most of my troubles are self-made hells. Why should I dump all my woes on the church? Then again, why not? Isn't that what You're there for? I'm a jerk with a conscience. What I mean is, going "back" to church is intimidating.

> The Lord is near to the brokenhearted
> and saves the crushed in spirit. (Ps 34:18)

I'm still here. And You're still listening. Thank You. Life is better than dreams. I'll get some wisdom. I'll go find a nun, a priest, a wise friend. Why not? I'll get some guidance.

I have a yearning. For prayer. For sacred traditions. For the cold silence of a church. For the gentle language that I learned. I spoke it. For the divine music that I heard. I sang it. Something is stirring inside me. God help me.

God of strength and peace You restore my soul.

Bibliography

Adalid, Jesús Sánchez. "Santa Teresa y la Inquisición: Femina inquieta, andariega, desobediente i contumaz, que a título de devoción inventaba malas dotrinas." *Clío: Revista de historia* 161 (2015) 52–57.

Barthes, Roland. *Sade, Fourier, Loyola* (English and French). Translated by Richard Miller. New York: Hill and Wang, 1976.

Birnbaum, Philip. *Maimonides' Code of Law and Ethics: Mishneh Torah.* Jerusalem: Hebrew, 1970.

Bloom, Anthony. *Beginning to Pray.* New York: Paulist, 1970.

Buber, Martin. *I and Thou.* Translated by Walter Kaufmann. New York: Scribner, 1971.

Chapman, Dom John. *Selected Letters.* London: Sheed and Ward, 1944.

Chardin, Teilhard de. *Le Milieu divin: Essai de vie intérieure.* Translated by B. J. Wall. London: Fontana, 1964.

Cranmer, Thomas. "Preface." In *Book of Common Prayer.* Cambridge: Cambridge University Press, 1979.

Danielou, Jean. *Prayer: The Mission of the Church*: Edinburgh: T. & T. Clark, 1996.

Douglas, Mary. *Purity and Danger.* London: Routledge and Paul, 1966.

Frere, Walter. *A New History of the Book of Common Prayer.* London: Macmillan, 1901.

Heaney, Seamus. "Clearances." In *Opened Ground: Selected Poems 1966–1996.* London: Faber and Faber, 1990.

Hooker, Richard. "A Learned and Comfortable Sermon of the Certainty and Perpetuity of Faith in the Elect." In *The Works Richard Hooker*, edited by John Keble. 3 vols. 1836. Revised by R. W. Church and F. Paget, 1888. Oxford: Franklin, 1970.

Hopkins, Gerard Manley. *The Collected Works of Gerard Manley Hopkins.* Oxford: Oxford University Press, 2013.

Kondo, Mari. *The Life-Changing Magic of Tidying Up: The Japanese Art of Decluttering and Organizing.* New York: Ten Speed, 2014.

Marcel, Gabriel. *The Mystery of Being.* Vol. 1, *Reflection and Mystery.* London: Harvill, 1950.

Bibliography

Nasr, Seyyed Hossain, et al. *The Study Quran: A New Translation and Commentary*. New York: HarperCollins, 2015.

Pasternak, Leonidovich Boris. *Doctor Zhivago*. Translated By Max Hayward and Manya Harari. London: Pantheon, 1958.

Rexroth, Kenneth. *With Eye and Ear*. New York: Herder and Herder, 1970.

Shakespeare, William. *The Complete Sonnets*. Edited by Colin Burrow. Oxford: Oxford University Press, 2010.

Shonkoff, Sam Berrin. "Metanomianism and Religious Praxis in Martin Buber's Hasidic Tales." *Religions* 9/12 (2018) 399. https://doi.org/10.3390/rel9120399.

Soskice, Janet Martin. *The Kindness of God: Metaphor, Gender, and Religious Language*. Oxford: Oxford University Press, 2007.

Unterman, Alan. *The Wisdom of the Jewish Mystics*. London: Sheldon, 1976.

Williams, Rowan. *Anglican Identities*. Oxford: Cowley, 2004.

———. "The Problem of Prayer (N146)." *Nomad Podcast*, May 24, 2017. https://www.nomadpodcast.co.uk/nomad-129-rowan-williams-problem-prayer/.

Weil, Simone. "Preface." In *Gravity and Grace*, translated by Emma Crawford and Mario von der Ruhr, 1–29. London: Routledge, 1952.

www.ingramcontent.com/pod-product-compliance
Lightning Source LLC
LaVergne TN
LVHW051708080426
835511LV00017B/2788